Mexican Americans

Hispanic Americans: Major Minority

Mexican Americans

Frank DePietro

Mason Crest

Mason Crest
370 Reed Road
Broomall, Pennsylvania 19008
www.masoncrest.com

Printed and bound in the United States of America.

First printing
9 8 7 6 5 4 3 2 1

Library of Congress Cataloging-in-Publication Data

DePietro, Frank.
 Mexican Americans / by Frank DePietro.
     p. cm.
 Includes index.
 ISBN 978-1-4222-2328-4 (hardcover) — ISBN 978-1-4222-2315-4 (series hardcover) — ISBN 978-1-4222-9332-4 (ebook)
 1. Mexican Americans—Juvenile literature. I. Title.
 E184.M5D46 2013
 973'.046872—dc23
                          2012010682

Produced by Harding House Publishing Services, Inc.
www.hardinghousepages.com
Cover design by Torque Advertising + Design.
Printed in USA.

Contents

Introduction

by José E. Limón, Ph.D.

Even before there was a United States, Hispanics were present in what would become this country. Beginning in the sixteenth century, Spanish explorers traversed North America, and their explorations encouraged settlement as early as the sixteenth century in what is now northern New Mexico and Florida, and as late as the mid-eighteenth century in what is now southern Texas and California.

Later, in the nineteenth century, following Spain's gradual withdrawal from the New World, Mexico in particular established its own distinctive presence in what is now the southwestern part of the United States, a presence reinforced in the first half of the twentieth century by substantial immigration from that country. At the close of the nineteenth century, the U.S. war with Spain brought Cuba and Puerto Rico into an interactive relationship with the United States, the latter in a special political and economic affiliation with the United States even as American power influenced the course of almost every other Latin American country.

The books in this series remind us of these historical origins, even as each explores the present reality of different Hispanic groups. Some of these books explore the contemporary social origins—what social scientists call the "push" factors—behind the accelerating Hispanic immigration to America: political instability, economic underdevelopment and crisis, environmental degradation, impoverished or wholly absent educational systems, and other circumstances contribute to many Latin Americans deciding they will be better off in the United States.

MEXICAN AMERICANS

And, for the most part, they will be. The vast majority come to work and work very hard, in order to earn better wages than they would back home. They fill significant labor needs in the U.S. economy and contribute to the economy through lower consumer prices and sales taxes.

When they leave their home countries, many immigrants may initially fear that they are leaving behind vital and important aspects of their home cultures: the Spanish language, kinship ties, food, music, folklore, and the arts. But as these books also make clear, culture is a fluid thing, and these native cultures are not only brought to America, they are also replenished in the United States in fascinating and novel ways. These books further suggest to us that Hispanic groups enhance American culture as a whole.

Our country—especially the young, future leaders who will read these books—can only benefit by the fair and full knowledge these authors provide about the socio-historical origins and contemporary cultural manifestations of America's Hispanic heritage.

Each chapter in this book opens with illustrations designed to resemble yarn paintings, a form of Mexican folk art.

chapter 1
Three Stories

George Elizondo is a boy with two names. His friends and teachers call him George. His parents usually call him George, too. But the older people in his family, his grandparents and aunts and uncles, call him Jorge (which sounds like "hore-hay"). That's what Mrs. Rivera, his mom's best friend, calls him. A lot of people at his church call him Jorge, too. He answers to both names—but he mostly thinks of himself as George.

George is one of millions of American kids whose **heritage** is Mexican. That's why he's called Jorge. Jorge is the Spanish name for George. George's parents and grandparents speak Spanish to each other. Spanish is the language of Mexico and the Mexican people. George can understand Spanish pretty well. He's not so good at speaking it. English is the language he knows best.

George and his family live in Rochester, New York. His mother's family comes from Santa Fe, in the state of New Mexico. They have lived there for as long as anyone can remember. George's great-great-great-grandfather owned a farm there. Today his Grandma and Grandpa Mendoza still live on the same land. His other grandparents, his father's parents, moved to California from Mexico. They became American **citizens**. All their children were born in the United States. George's parents met in college. They moved to New York State when George was a baby. Most summers, the Elizondos travel west to visit their family. When George is in California and New Mexico, it seems like almost everyone calls him Jorge!

A **heritage** i
something t
was passed
down to you
your parents
grandparen
THEIR paren
grandparen

Citizens are
people who
in a country
have the rig
vote, as wel
other rights.

Mexicans shopping in a grocery store in Tijuana.

Sometimes, his Grandma Elizondo tells him stories about Mexico and what it was like to grow up there. George likes to hear his grandma's stories. But George thinks of himself as a plain-old American, not a Mexican American. As he's gotten older, though, he's started to learn more about his Mexican heritage. He loves the food, the stories, and the old songs his grandmother sings. "Being Mexican makes us strong," his grandfather told him once. "We aren't like anyone else."

George isn't sure he agrees; he thinks he's pretty much like most everyone else he knows. But he's proud of all the people in his family. He's proud of Grandpa Mendoza's family who lived on their land for hundreds of years. And he's proud of Grandma Elizondo's family who were brave enough to start a new life in another country. He's proud of his Mexican heritage.

Another Story

Lupe Ortega grew up in Mexico City. Her mother sold fruit on the sidewalks. Her father sold gum and candy bars. The Ortega family was very poor. When Lupe's family lived in Mexico, their home was just one room in an old building. It was dark and crowded. One side of the building had fallen down during a big earthquake that happened before

Lupe was born. Home in those days was a noisy place where you could never be alone. Lots of other kids lived in the building too. Lupe and her sister, Pepita, always had someone to play with.

But they never had very much to eat. Their parents were out working all the time, trying to make money. Lupe and Pepita were on their own most of the time. Sometimes the girls begged their parents to stay home with them. But they knew if their mother and father didn't work all day, every day, they wouldn't be able to pay the rent or buy food. Life was very hard for the Ortega family.

Sometimes, Lupe would tell her little sister stories about going to live with Uncle Pedro and Aunt Elena in the United States. They both dreamed of being able to go and live there. Lupe's aunt and uncle had been living in the United States for years. Uncle Pedro had a job in a factory in Chicago. He and his family had a nice house with three bedrooms, a living room, and a kitchen. They even had another room in their basement where Lupe's cousins played games and watched television. Her aunt and uncle had invited Lupe's family to come stay with them so they could become Americans too.

Many Mexican Americans live in New Mexico where their families have lived for centuries.

Mexico City

The Ortegas had put their names on a list to allow them to move to the United States. The list was very long. They had to wait their turn. They had been waiting so long that Lupe didn't believe they would ever really leave Mexico.

Finally, though, everything changed for the Ortegas. Their names were on the list of people who could enter the United States. Uncle Pedro sent them money for the airplane. They flew all the way to Chicago, Illinois.

Now, Lupe lives with her family in a house with two bedrooms. Her father works in the factory where Uncle Pedro works. Her mother works in a store. The whole family is learning English. They are working hard to become American citizens. Lupe knows her family doesn't have as much money as a lot of the other kids at her school. But she still remembers what it was like when her whole family lived in one room. She feels sad and angry when other kids make fun of the way she talks or the way she dresses. Sometimes she's homesick for the kids she grew up with back in Mexico City. But Lupe and her family are very happy to be in the United States. They know if they work hard they can live a much better life here.

Mexico is full of children whose parents are too poor to care for them.

Homeless camp in Tijuana

A Third Story

Pancho Espinoza grew up in a garbage dump. He and his parents and brothers and sisters lived in a little shack made from plastic garbage bags, a few old pieces of plywood, and a cardboard box. His family spent their whole day looking through the garbage for things to sell and use. They lived on the stuff that other people in the city of Tijuana threw out. They wore clothes from the dump. They even found their food there. What Pancho liked best was finding what he thought of as treats: half-rotten fruit and packages of stale, sweet cookies.

MEXICAN AMERICANS

Tijuana is full of desperately poor people. This overflow duct for the Tijuana River is home to several families.

THE CITY OF TIJUANA

Tijuana is a city right on the border between Mexico and California. Tijuana is constantly growing. As many as 65,000 people are added to its population every year. Many of these people move to Tijuana from other parts of Mexico. They come to the city to find jobs in factories and the tourist business. The city is growing by about eight acres a day!

The city's housing, roads, running water, and other public services can't keep up with how fast it is growing. Some poor families get electricity by hooking up illegal lines that can cause fires. When your house is made from cardboard and plywood, a fire can wipe out everything you own in just a few minutes.

It was the only life Pancho had ever known. He never expected it to change. But when he was eleven, everything fell apart for his family. His father got sick. They had no money to take him to the doctor. Finally, Pancho's father died.

Without him, the family became even poorer. His older brothers began selling drugs to make money. His mother could not earn enough money to keep them all fed. She brought Pancho and his little brother to an orphanage.

The orphanage was filled with other boys like Pancho and his brother. None of them were really orphans. They came from very poor families

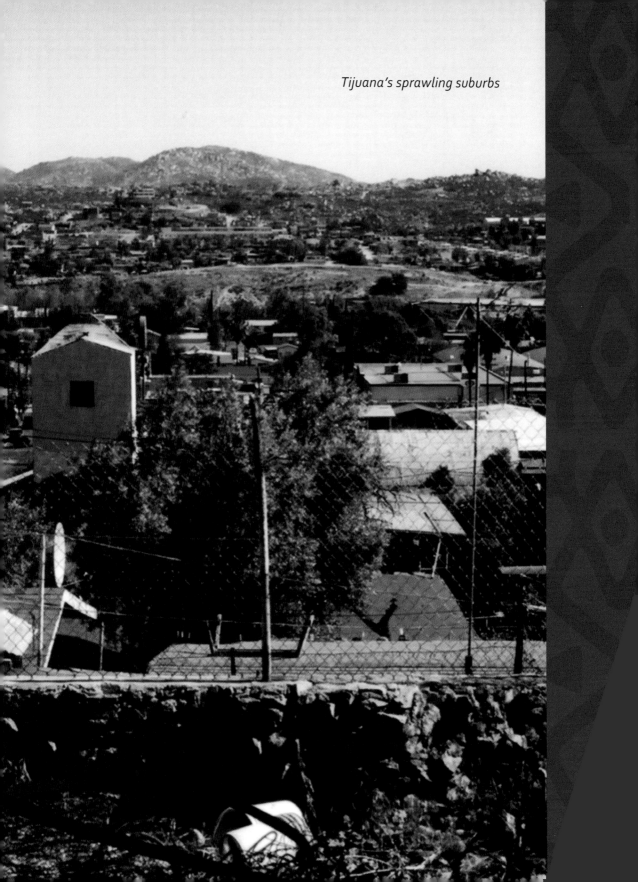

Tijuana's sprawling suburbs

where the parents could not take care of all their children. Pancho was angry that his sisters got to stay with his mother. He was angry with the orphanage workers. He was angry he wasn't old enough to take care of himself like his big brothers.

As soon as Pancho was old enough to get a job, he ran away from the orphanage. On a dark night, he crossed the border to the United States. Border Patrol officers almost caught him. He cut his face on the barbed-wire fence that marked the line between Mexico and the United States. Bleeding and scared, he made his way to Los Angeles.

Pancho still lives in Los Angeles. He has a wife and children of his own now. His wife works as a maid in a rich family's home. He works as a mechanic in a garage. He still has a deep scar across his face where the barbed wire tore his skin.

Pancho works hard. He and his family live a much better life in the United States than they ever could have in a Mexican garbage dump. They may not be rich by American standards—but they don't earn their living from picking through other people's trash. They have enough money to take care of their own children. They are proud of their family.

But Pancho lives here illegally. He broke the law when he snuck across the border from Mexico without the right papers. If he was ever caught, he will be sent back to Mexico. If he ever got into any kind of trouble, he could lose everything he has worked so hard for. As an **illegal immigrant**, he could forced to leave the United States at any time.

All Mexican Americans

George Elizondo, Lupe Ortega, and Pancho Espinoza are all Mexican Americans. Like every other Mexican American, they have their own stories. Some have lived on the land that is now America's Southwest for

MEXICAN AMERICANS

This boy lives in an orphanage while his parents are in prison.

Children in Mexico dragging a bin of garbage.

TRASH ECONOMY

Every day, about 1,200 tons of trash is carried into the Tijuana dump by giant trucks. The people who make their living in the dump earn between $100 and $150 a month from the things they pull out of the garbage to sell. It is a hard and dangerous life.

Most people who live in Mexican dumps live much shorter lives than other Mexicans. Diseases are very common. The dumps are filled with dangerous germs. Poisonous chemicals are also in the garbage. These killer poisons end up in the trash people's eyes, skin, and blood.

Many people who live there can't get better jobs. They come from the poorest families. They have never gone to school. They don't know how to escape the dump.

hundreds of years. Others are more recent immigrants whose families moved north looking for jobs and safety. Some are here legally; some aren't. But almost all are hardworking people who give a lot to our country. They help make the United States a richer and more interesting place!

chapter 2
Two Worlds

The people of modern Mexico have a long and very interesting history. Until about 500 years ago, **Native** people (the people we sometimes call "Indians") had Mexico all to themselves. For thousands of years they hunted and fished and gathered plants to eat. Later, they were the first people in the world to grow corn, beans, tomatoes, chili peppers, and cocoa. Their villages grew into cities. Chiefs became kings. The ancient Mexicans worked in gold, pottery, and beautiful cloth. They built great stone pyramids for their gods. The great **empire** of the Aztecs was at its largest and most powerful when the Spanish first came to Mexico.

We all know the date 1492. In that year, Christopher Columbus—an Italian sailing in ships owned by Spain—crossed the Atlantic Ocean and "discovered" America. Of course he didn't really discover a new continent. Millions of people already lived here! But before Columbus landed, the people on both sides of the Atlantic Ocean—the Natives on this side and the Europeans on the other—knew nothing about each other.

Columbus thought he had landed in India. He called the Natives "Indians." Even though people knew that North America and South America weren't India, the name "Indian" stuck for centuries. Even today, people call the Native Americans Indians. This can be pretty confusing since there are also people around who really ARE from India!

Native means someone was b particular place

An empire is m countries or lar controlled by a ruler (an emper

A TERRIBLE NUMBER

No one knows for sure how many Native people died after the Europeans' came—but it was probably around 40 million people who died in the first 100 years. Imagine if ALL the people in the country of Canada were to die—or ALL the people in the U.S. state of California. That would be about the same number of people.

uistador *is a
sh word that
"conqueror."
use it to
the Spanish
ers who came
Americas and
ered the Native
who lived there.*

Anyway, Columbus claimed the land for Spain. He didn't pay any attention to the fact that people were already living on the land. He didn't think these people were quite as real as European people with white skins. In fact, he wrote that he thought the Natives would make good slaves.

Columbus and the many Spaniards that later crossed the Atlantic came to New Spain to get rich. Almost all of the meetings between Spaniards and Natives after 1492 were very unfriendly. The Spanish claimed the Native's land and took whatever they wanted. The Natives fought bravely for their homes. But their bows and arrows were no match for Spanish horsemen with guns and cannons.

Wherever they went, the Spanish **conquistadors** searched for gold. They took the Native people as slaves. Over the next two hundred years, millions of Natives died in wars with the Spanish. They also died from diseases brought from Europe. It was a terrible time for the Native people of America.

Moctezuma, Cortés, and the Aztec Kingdom

The Aztec were a rich and powerful people. For hundreds of years they ruled over what is now Mexico. They were great warriors. They had built their kingdom by conquering tribes all over Mexico. They were also great artists. They worked in gold, pottery, and colorful cloth. And they were builders of great cities. When the Spanish came to America the Aztec's most important city was one of the largest in the whole world. It was a beautiful city built out over a huge lake. The Aztecs called their great city Tenochtitlan (tee-nock-teet-lan). The city had palaces and markets and thousands of houses. At the center of the city were huge stone pyramids. Here the Aztecs prayed to their gods.

Hernán Cortés and his conquistadors rode into Tenochtitlan in 1519. They were amazed by the size and wealth of the city. No city in Spain was as big or as beautiful. They met with the great king of the Aztecs, Moctezuma. Thousands of rich

Aztec drawing of the founding of Tenochtitlan

Aztec warriors

THE OLMECS

The Aztecs were not the first people to live in Mexico. Before the Aztecs, the Olmecs lived there for thousands of years, since 2000 BCE. The Olmecs had systems of numbering, writing, and keeping track of weeks and months. They also invented things we still use today. For example, North America's favorite sport—basketball—comes from the rubber-ball game played by these ancient people.

and beautifully dressed Aztecs gathered for this meeting. Moctezuma gave Cortés a necklace of solid gold.

The Aztecs of Tenochtitlan had never seen people like the conquistadors. The white-skinned men wore armor that shone in the sun. They rode on animals that looked like giant deer. They had hairy faces ... and they had guns. Some of the Aztecs thought the Spanish might be gods that had come to earth. At first, the Aztec just wanted to make these strangers happy.

The Spanish were greedy for everything they saw. They were willing to fight to get it. Over the next few months, Cortés and his conquistadors conquered the Aztec kingdom. Old enemies of the Aztecs joined with the Spanish to make a mighty army. This army is said to have had 200,000 warriors!

The Aztec warriors were very brave. They knew they were fighting to save their people's land. There were many bloody battles. Moctezuma was taken prisoner.

Depiction of an Aztec ceremony

Meanwhile, a disease called smallpox spread through the kingdom. Thousands and thousands of Aztecs died from war and disease. It was a time of terror and death for the Native people of Mexico. By the end of 1520, the great city of the Aztecs had been destroyed. Moctezuma and many other Aztec leaders were dead. The riches and power of the whole Aztec kingdom now belonged to the Spanish.

The great Aztecs became a conquered people. The rule of the Spanish was hard. They did not care about the old Aztec ways. The Spanish wanted as much gold as they could get. They wanted more land and more slaves. They were in Mexico to stay.

But there were still millions of Native people in Mexico. Somehow the Spanish and the Natives would have to learn to live together. While thousands of people were dying, there were still babies being born. Some of these babies had Spanish fathers and Native mothers. Captain Cortés himself was the father of one of these babies. They would grow up to be a

MEXICAN AMERICANS

Aztec ruins

Modern view of Mexico City

THE REBIRTH OF THE CITY OF MEXICO

A new city, named Mexico City, was built in the same place as Tenochtitlan. Many of the stones from the old city were used to build the new one. Today 20 million people live in Mexico City. It is again one of the greatest cities in the world!

new people, part Native and part Spanish. They would learn Spanish ways from their fathers. Their mothers would teach them the old ways of the Native people. And that mixture of Native and Spanish **culture** and people would make a new Mexico!

*The word **culture** means the customs and beliefs of a group of people.*

A New Religion for Mexico

The Spanish people were Christians. They believed Christianity was the only true way for people to worship God. The Spanish who came to the New World wanted to make all the Native people become Catholic. That was almost as important to them as finding gold! The Native people of Mexico had their own religion. But the Spanish believed the Native religions were all wrong. They did not care what the Natives believed. The Christian religion would be the only religion allowed in Mexico. They forced the Natives of Mexico to give up their old religions. They made them become Christians. The Natives were not given a choice.

DO YOU LIKE TACOS?

Most American kids love tacos! This tasty food came from Mexico. It is a very, very old recipe. Mexican people brought tacos to America. Like the Mexican people, tacos are a great mix of native and Spanish things mixed together. The tortilla, the taco shell, is made from native corn. The beef in the filling is Spanish. (If you like beans in your taco, they're native, too.) The cheese on top is Spanish. The salsa is both native and Spanish. The tomatoes and chili peppers are native. The onions are Spanish. All together they make something special and delicious. Next time you eat a taco think about the wonderful history of the Mexican people. Think about how mixing things from two different continents made something new. Think about how great that mix can be!

The conquistadors traveled with Catholic priests. Together, the conquistadors and the priests built churches wherever they went. Sometimes the priests would stay behind to teach the conquered people the new religion. Most of the Spanish did not care about the Native people. They only wanted their gold and their land. But some of the priests really did love the Natives. They taught them that the Christian God loved them, too. They sometimes took the Native's side against the Spanish rulers. They tried to help them.

MEXICAN AMERICANS

The Spanish priests worked to bring
Christianity to Native people.

33

Church in Mexico

34

It was very hard for the Aztecs to give up their old religions. They believed in their old gods. They believed in their old ways of praying. Most of the Natives became Christians because they had to, not because they wanted to. They had lost their land to the Spanish. Their riches had been taken from them. Many of their friends and family had died of European diseases. Their cities and towns had been destroyed. It was a time of great sadness for the Native people of Mexico. They had lost their hope for the future.

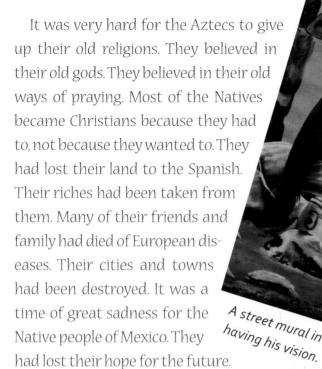

A street mural in Tijuana records Juan Diego having his vision.

Could the Christian religion help them? Could it bring the Spanish people and the Native people together? Would it ever bring the peace the Christian priests promised?

A Vision of Hope— and a New People

Juan Diego was a poor Native man. One December morning in 1531 he was walking in the hills outside Mexico City. Maybe he was feeling sad about his people and all the changes they had had to face.

Suddenly he saw a beautiful woman surrounded by light. She spoke to Juan Diego in his own Native language. She was dark-skinned like the Native people. She told him she was Mary, the mother of Jesus Christ. She said she understood how hard things were for the Native people. She promised him she would always love and care for the people of Mexico.

The Virgin's image appears in many places throughout Mexico and the United States.

LA RAZA

Today, many Mexican Americans speak of "la Raza," a word that means all the people who are a mix of Spanish and Native heritage. It is a term of pride in the past and hope for the future.

She would watch over them. If they believed in her, they would always have hope for the future. She asked that a beautiful church be built on the spot where she appeared that day. She wanted the people of Mexico to always remember her.

Juan Diego told his story to the Spanish priests. They did not believe him. But a **miracle** took place! On the inside of the coat Juan Diego was wearing was a beautiful picture of Mary, just as she had appeared to him.

A great church was built on the hill where Juan Diego had seen her. The place was called Guadalupe. People from all over Mexico, both Natives and Spanish, came to this church to pray together. Our Lady of Guadalupe became a **symbol** of God's love and care for the people of Mexico and the Americas. Both the Natives and the Spanish loved her.

The Spanish-speaking people of the Americas still love her. They believe she has watched over them and loved them for hundreds of years, just like a mother would. Millions of people still visit her church in Mexico every year. The look at the image of her on Juan Diego's cloak. This image

*A **miracle** is something amazing that happens, usually because God made it happen.*

*A **symbol** is something that stands for something else.*

of Our Lady, a beautiful Native woman in blue, surrounded by light, is seen all over Mexico and wherever Mexican people live.

The Christian religion was brought to the New World by the Spanish. But now it became the religion of the Mexican people, too. It brought the Spanish and the Natives closer together. It helped make them one people with one God. Mexico is still a very Catholic country. In many cities and towns the church is the largest and most beautiful building of all. The Catholic religion and the mixture of Native and Spanish families created a new people.

It was as a new people that Natives and Spaniards faced the future. The Mexican people were now a rich mixture of people and culture. Their religion was a mix of Native and Spanish ideas. Their delicious food mixed Native and European cuisine.

A modern mural of the Virgin of Guadalupe portrays her holding a child dead from street violence.

MEXICAN AMERICANS

Mexico and the United States

In the 1800s, the people of Mexico fought the Spanish to become their own country. Much of the land that had been part of Mexico—what is now California, Texas, and New Mexico—ended up becoming part of the United State. But the Mexican people who lived there often stayed on the same land. Even though they were Mexicans, now they lived in the United States.

Other people of the United States and Mexico moved back and forth across the border. The United States was a big and rich country. Many Mexican people who wanted to make better lives for themselves moved there from further south. They were looking for jobs and homes. They were looking were looking for a land where they could raise their children.

The ancient land of the early Mexicans.

chapter 3
A People Willing to Work

The United States is a nation of immigrants. Unless you are 100 percent Native American, your ancestors came to this country from somewhere else. People from Italy, England, Ireland, China, and India—people from all parts of the world—have come here to make a new life. African Americans, many brought here as slaves, add to the mix. The promise of America to all its people, immigrants old and new, is one of freedom and **opportunity** for all.

Some Mexican-American families have been here for hundreds of years. Some have just come to the United States. Many Mexican Americans have been very successful in the United States. But like almost all immigrant groups, they had to start at the bottom and work very hard.

The flow of Mexican immigrants looking for work in the United States is not new. For the past hundred years Mexican Americans have been a big part of the American **workforce**.

During World War I and World War II, the American government brought thousands of Mexicans into the United States. They were brought in as temporary farm workers to replace American workers who had gone to war. These Mexican workers were not treated very well. They were not paid a fair amount for their work. Despite this, many of these workers did not return to Mexico after the war. Many of them traveled from one place to another, picking crops as they ripened across

> An **opportunity** is a chance to do something.
>
> **Workforce** means all the people who have jobs.

ILLEGAL IMMIGRANTS

There may be as many as 11 million illegal immigrants in the United States. Over half of them are people who have come to the United States from Mexico. From the 1950s through the 1980s, most of these illegal aliens found work as farm workers. Today, many illegal Mexican immigrants work in hotels, restaurants, car washes, and health-care centers. They work hard at jobs that most other Americans don't want. They are a poorly paid but very important part of the American workforce.

nt workers
ople who move
' the country,
arm work
y picking fruit
getables).

gling *means*
ng something
t permission.

the country. American farmers came to depend on these **migrant workers** to do a lot of the work on their farms. The pay was low and the work was very hard. As more and more farmland was created in the western United States (7.5 million acres between 1945 and 1955), more and more farm workers were needed. **Smuggling** illegal workers into the United States became a big business. It still is.

For many years, new Mexican immigrants settled into older Mexican communities in the southwest United States. Cities like Los Angeles in California, Albuquerque in New Mexico, and San Antonio in Texas had started out being Mexican, before they became part of the United States. These old communities have kept their strong Mexican heritage. New immigrants helped keep the Spanish language, the Catholic faith, and old Mexican ways alive. Many Mexican Americans moved up into the middle class. Some became very successful.

Many Mexican Americans still live in the states that border Mexico. In some communities, people of Mexican heritage are in the **majority**. But Mexican Americans have moved all over the United States. They have made homes for themselves in towns and cities across America. New immigrants, legal and illegal, continue to cross the border. Many of these new immigrants work very hard in low-paying jobs that other Americans don't want to do. Some American citizens have bad feelings about these workers who come across the border. They are afraid that Mexican

> **Majority** *means that there is more of something than there is of anything else.*

Young Mexican men like these often head to the other side of the border.

A People Willing to Work 43

COYOTES

People who make their living smuggling Mexicans into the United States are called coyotes. These coyotes charge people a lot of money to get them across the border. They have systems of trucks and buses, secret hideouts, fake legal papers, and guides. The trip can be very dangerous. And some coyotes are dishonest people. Truckloads of illegal immigrants have been found dead in the desert. They suffocated in crowded vehicles without fresh air or water.

U.S.-Mexico border

Workers unite in Tijuana to march in protest of their low-paying jobs.

Mexican carrot pickers in California during the first half of the twentieth century.

workers will take jobs away from Americans during a time when there are not enough jobs to go around. But most experts agree that Mexican workers are very good for America.

Mexican immigrants continue to face **prejudice** in the Unites States. Americans have always had **stereotypes** of Mexicans. They think all Mexicans are lazy. The picture of a Mexican in a big sombrero taking a nap beneath a cactus is one that most Americans have seen. The truth is very different. A lot of America's wealth has come from the hard work and energy of Mexican workers. Prejudice is a hard enemy to fight. But today, more and more Mexican Americans have learned to take pride in their communities. They know they have given a lot to our country.

Prejudice *is judg a group of peopl unfairly, based o race or religion (o something else c them).*

Stereotypes *are simple, false ide about a person b on the group to that person belo People who belie stereotypes thin that every indivi in a particular gr is just like everyo else in that grou, Stereotypes arer true!*

chapter 4
A Name of Their Own

Many Americans of Mexican heritage call themselves Chicanos. (Chicana is the female form of the word.) It is a very old word. It goes back to the name the long-ago Aztec people called themselves. Years ago, the word was used as an insult in Mexico. It meant a low-class person. Mexican Americans took the insult and made it into a word of pride. Now it is a name that many Mexican Americans choose for themselves. It reminds them of their heritage in Mexico. It makes them feel proud to be who they are.

The word "Chicano" came out of the **civil rights** movements of the 1960s and '70s. African Americans were speaking out for their rights. Many Mexican Americans did, too. The Chicano Rights Movement worked to teach Mexican Americans about their rich history and heritage. It supported art, music, and writing by Mexican Americans. It fought against prejudice and stereotypes. The movement helped build pride in the past and hope for the future in Mexican American communities.

The Chicano Movement had many heroes—community leaders, **activists**, artists, and teachers. Leaders such as Reis Lopes Tijerina, Corky González, César Chávez, and Dolores Huerta gave the movement a voice. They called attention to the problems facing Chicanos. They made the whole country listen!

Civil rights are freedom and eq that all human deserve.

Activists are p who are willing action to bring change for the

César Chávez

The Chicano Movement did not end in the 1960s and '70s. It continues today. Education is very important to the movement. It supports Mexican American students. It helped start many **bilingual-bicultural** programs in schools. The arts are also very important to the movement. Painting, music, dance, writing, and theater are ways Chicanos show pride in their heritage. Art has taught many other Americans a lot about Mexican Americans. American music, art, language, food, fashion, politics, and lifestyle are being shaped by the rich heritage of Chicanos.

Unfortunately, prejudice against Mexican Americans still exists. But more and more Mexican Americans are learning to be very proud of who they are. And other Americans are learning from them!

Bilingual *has to do with speaking two languages.*

Bicultural *has to do with two different cultures.*

CÉSAR CHÁVEZ AND DOLORES HUERTA

César Chávez was a Mexican American who grew up working on farms in California. Farm workers worked hard in sometimes dangerous conditions. Their pay was very low. César wanted to make things better. He helped start labor unions for farm workers. This helped the workers get higher pay and better working conditions from the farm owners. In 1962, César Chávez and another activist, Dolores Huerta, started the National Farm Workers Association (NFWA). Later, they also started the United Farm Workers' Organizing Committee (UFWOC). Under the leadership of César Chávez and Dolores Huerta, the UFWOC organized marches and protests to fight for better working conditions. People all across America listened to them. César and Dolores helped make things better for Mexican American workers.

Famous Mexican Americans

Entertainment

Mario López: actor

George Lopez: actor, comedian

Jimmy Smits: actor

Paul Rodriguez: comedian

Carlos Santana: musician

Lila Downs: singer

Linda Ronstadt: singer

Selena: singer

Sports

Oscar de la Hoya: boxing

Rudy Galindo: figure skating

Nancy Lopez: golf

Lee Trevino: golf

George Lopez

Oscar de la Hoya

Politics

Kenneth Salazar: Secretary of the Interior

Henry Cisneros: former Secretary of Housing and Urban Development

Bill Richardson: governor of New Mexico

Activists

César Chávez: labor union organizer

Linda Chávez-Thompson: labor union organizer

Dolores Huerta: labor union organizer

Authors

Sandra Cisneros: author

Rubén Salazar: author, journalist

Astronaut and Scientist

Ellen Ochoa: astronaut

Mario Molina: Nobel Prize–winning chemist

Cultural Wealth and Economic Poverty

Mexican American culture has made life in America richer for everybody. In sports and entertainment, in food and music, in politics and education—Chicanos are a very important part of American life.

Mexican Americans have a heritage that goes back to the Aztecs and the conquistadors of Spain. They have a strong faith in God. They take comfort in the protection of Our Lady of Guadalupe. They have created beautiful works of art. They have been successful in many, many things. The Chicano Movement has helped Mexican Americans value their own culture. It has helped all Americans understand what Chicanos have to offer our country.

But Mexican Americans still have a way to go. Poverty and prejudice are still a part of many Mexican Americans' lives. Many Mexican Americans are living well, but many are not.

More than one in four Mexican Americans lives in poverty. The number is probably much higher if you include "illegal" Mexican Americans (people who are in the United States without the American government's permission).

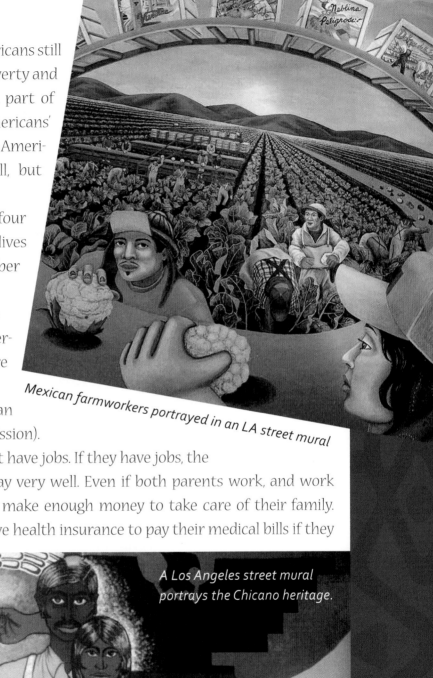

Mexican farmworkers portrayed in an LA street mural

Many Chicanos don't have jobs. If they have jobs, the jobs usually don't pay very well. Even if both parents work, and work hard, they may not make enough money to take care of their family. Most Americans have health insurance to pay their medical bills if they

A Los Angeles street mural portrays the Chicano heritage.

A Mexican American celebrates his heritage with a traditional Native costume.

get sick or hurt. Only 20 percent of Mexican Americans have health insurance. This means if they or their children get sick, they may not be able to afford to go to a doctor. They may not have money to pay for medicine.

A lot of Mexican kids don't see much of a future for themselves. They have watched their parents work hard and get nowhere. Many Chicano kids drop out of high school. Drugs and gangs are big problems in many poor Chicano communities. Gang membership leads to violence. Many gang members end up in jail. And prejudice against Mexicans holds people back.

Progress is being made. But that progress is slow. When there aren't enough jobs to go around, poor people can get left behind.

But the Mexican American community is growing fast. More and more Mexican Americans are becoming successful in the United States. They will be a very big part of American culture in the twenty-first century. Hopefully, all Mexican Americans will have more chances to take advantage of all America has to offer. At the same time, the rest of America has a lot to learn from Mexican Americans. And a lot to thank them for!

Time Line

1100 Mayan Civilization is at its strongest in Central America.

1325 Aztecs conquer Mexico.

1438 Inca rule begins in Peru.

1492 Christopher Columbus lands on the island of Hispaniola (Santo Domingo and Haiti).

1503 Hernán Cortés arrives in Hispaniola.

1521 Cortés defeats the Aztecs in Mexico.

1532 Francisco Pizarro conquers the Inca in Peru.

1610 Santa Fe, New Mexico, is built.

1690 First Spanish settlement in Texas is built.

1769 Franciscan missionary Junípero Serra builds the first mission in California. He will eventually build ten missions up and down California.

1817 Simón Bolívar begins his fight for independence from Spain in Colombia, Venezuela, and Ecuador.

1821 Mexico declares independence from Spain.

1845 Texas becomes part of the United States.

1846 Mexican-American War begins. New Mexico (which includes modern-day New Mexico, Arizona, southern Colorado, southern Utah, and southern Utah) becomes part of the United States.

1868 The Fourteenth Amendment to the U.S. Constitution says that all Hispanics born in the United States are U.S. citizens.

1898 Puerto Rico and Cuba become part of the United States.

1901 Cuba becomes an independent country.

1902 The Reclamation Act is passed, and takes away land from many Hispanic Americans.

1910 The beginning of the Mexican Revolution sends thousands of Mexicans north to settle in the American Southwest.

1943 U.S. government allows Mexican farmworkers to enter the United States.

1959 Fidel Castro takes over Cuba. Many Cubans immigrate to the United States.

1970s Violence in Central America spurs massive migration to the United States.

1990 President George Bush appoints the first woman and first Hispanic surgeon general of the United States: Antonia C. Novello.

2003 Hispanics are pronounced the nation's largest minority group surpassing African Americans—after new Census figures are released showing the U.S. Hispanic population at 37.1 million as of July 2001.

2006 According to the Census Bureau, the number of Hispanic-owned businesses grew three times faster than the national average for all U.S. businesses.

Find Out More

IN BOOKS

Hernandez, Roger E. and Hunter, Amy N. *History of Mexico*. Philadelphia, Pa.: Mason Crest, 2002.

Jovinelly, Joann and Jason Netelkos. *Crafts and Culture of the Aztecs*. New York: Rosen Publishing Group, 2003.

Sanna, Ellyn. *Mexican American, American Regional Cooking Library*. Philadelphia, Pa.: Mason Crest, 2004.

Stokes, Erica M. and Roger E. Hernandez. *Economy of Mexico.* Philadelphia, Pa.: Mason Crest, 2002.

ON THE INTERNET

Mexican Embassy
www.mexican-embassy.dk

MEXonline
www.mexonline.com/cultart.htm

Mexican independence
www.tamu.edu/ccbn/dewitt/mexicanrev.htm

Mexico Connect Time Line Overview
www.mexconnect.com/mex_/history.html

Picture Credits

Benjamin Stewart: p. 10, 11, 13, 15, 17, 19, 39, 43, 45

Corel: p. 56

Czuber | Dreamstime.com: p. 14

DEWALT POWER TOOLS FIGHT NIGHT CLUB 2010: p. 53

Guillermo Lopez | Dreamstime.com: p. 12

Hector Fernandez | Dreamstime.com: p. 30

Jerl71 | Dreamstime.com: p. 29

Joel Levine: p. 50

Library of Congress: p. 46

Michelle Bouch: p. 8, 22, 40, 48

Millaus | Dreamstime.com: p. 20

Patrick Poendl | Dreamstime.com: p. 44

PhotoDisc: p. 25, 26

Photos.com: p. 33

Sergey Gelman | Dreamstime.com: p. 28

Stephan Scherhag | Dreamstime.com: p. 34

Turkbug | Dreamstime.com: p. 52

To the best knowledge of the publisher, all other images are in the public domain. If any image has been inadvertently uncredited, please notify Harding House Publishing Services, Vestal, New York 13850, so that rectification can be made for future printings.

MEXICAN AMERICANS

Index

About the Author and the Consultant

Frank DePietro is an editor and author who lives in Upstate New York. He studied anthropology in college, and he continues to be fascinated with the world's cultures, art, and folklore.

Dr. José E. Limón is professor of Mexican-American Studies at the University of Texas at Austin where he has taught for twenty-five years. He has authored over forty articles and three books on Latino cultural studies and history. He lectures widely to academic audiences, civic groups, and K–12 educators.